D1299636

# MEDITATIONS FOR SUCCESS

# MEDITATIONS FOR

# SUCCESS

## BY ANNIE ZINKER AND LEAH KRAVAT

WINGS BOOKS ■ NEW YORK ■ NEW JERSEY

Random House
New York • Toronto • London • Sydney • Auckland

Jacket art: On the Points, Wassily Kandinsky
Design: Nora Sheehan
Production supervision by Roméo Enriquez

**Printed and bound in Mexico**

Library of Congress Cataloging-in-Publication Data

Zinker, Annie.
Meditations for success / by Annie Zinker and Leah Kravat.
p.      cm.
ISBN 0-517-12416-5 (hardcover)
1. Success—Psychological aspects.   2. Meditation.   I. Kravat, Leah.
II. Title.

BF637.S8Z56   1995                                              95-8668
158'.1—dc20                                                          CIP

8   7   6   5   4   3   2   1

ABOUT THE AUTHORS

Leah Kravat is a writer who was born and raised in New York City. She continues her career in the fitness field while pursuing writing and, when weather permits, star gazing.

Annie Zinker is a psychotherapist practicing in New York City, mother of five children, grandmother, athlete and writer who is inspired by life in the city and by the peaceful quiet of Southampton.

*Something we were withholding made us weak,*
*Until we found it was ourselves.*
ROBERT FROST

We have been asked to write a book of meditations on success. We are afraid to tell our friends and family about this project for fear that they will laugh, or, at the very least, roll their eyes in wonder and shock. What do we know about meditations except for that which we have read and practiced ourselves? What do we know about success? Isn't this a somewhat grandiose project for a psychotherapist and a fledgling writer? The answer of course is yes. ▪ When we first think about it, the project looms over us like Mount Everest. Must we climb it because it's there? Couldn't we simply say, "No thank you, we're too busy just now," not make the effort and not risk failure and ridicule? The answer to that question is also yes. ▪ And what do we really know of the nature of success? Well, we have survived childhood and school, had careers, borne children, planted flowers and tomatoes, overcome certain of life's vicissitudes, loved and been loved. ▪ Despite ourselves, our inhibitions and uncertainties, the process is taking place. Perhaps, as Aristotle said, "The starting point seems to be stronger when reason is disengaged." And so it is with us. A spark has touched some source within us that enables us to reach beyond what we thought we knew—or didn't know—to discover a light that burns in us all. ▪ We thank our editor, the authors on whom we have relied for inspiration, and God for making us aware of the untouched, previously unexperienced corners of our souls and hearts. We hope that others will also reach inside and find their own unexpected and surprising corners of light—and of course meditate on what they find there.

— ANNIE & LEAH

GARDEN OF THE CHATEAU, PAUL KLEE

*True success is therefore the experience of the miraculous. It is the unfolding of the divinity within us.*
DEEPAK CHOPRA

n our meditations we seek new pathways to self-knowledge, releasing our thoughts from past constraints, freeing our minds to achieve a deeper, wider understanding, and with that, acceptance and serenity.  We embrace success as a journey, not a destination, and as such will contemplate some stops along the way. The more idealistic, perhaps obvious manifestations of success are those represented by life's simple pleasures, like taking time out from a busy schedule to enjoy a summer day, watch our children grow, help another and, from time-to-time, become aware of our own growth, noting the changes in our perceptions, sensitivity, spirituality and courage. In addition, we consider some of success' more tangible trappings—money, material possessions, job titles—perhaps viewing them in a different way, from the inside.  There is darkness as well as light in our universe; the darkness challenges us to battle and the light guides our spirituality. It seems that our crimes against our loved ones and our enemies are present as often as the good we attempt to do. But to deny the existence and energy of anger, revenge, envy and sorrow, would be as foolish as to deny the power of love and generosity of spirit.  Thus, cowardice, greed, avarice and all our other ugly character traits, are as worthy of our attention as are the nobler qualities to which we all, somewhere in our souls, aspire. Let us embrace this and strive *not* for success in our meditations, but rather for deeper and greater understanding of *all* that moves heaven and earth—and ourselves.

LARGE LANDSCAPE, PIET MONDRIAN

*A minute's success pays the failure of years.*
ROBERT BROWNING

I f you ask a thousand people, you'll hear a thousand different interpretations of the word *success*. To some it is a glorious, beautiful gift, simple and sweet, that lifts the spirit. But to others it can feel like a rough, heavy burden, something that weighs them down. We each experience success differently. For instance, do we view it as an internal experience or as an external occurrence? Is it a feeling, something private and personal, or a concrete thing, something we can point to with pride and expect others to see and value as we do? Clearly our differing interpretations have much to do with whatever personal criteria govern our goals and aspirations. If the opposite of success were failure, which of the thousand ways would we choose to define *that* state of being? What would failure look like to each of us? Is there a particular place on any measuring device that marks the "failure" spot or the "success" spot, as one might, for example, find the freezing point on a thermometer, or the pound mark on a scale? We understand that the space between black and white has countless shades of gray and we would be hard put to determine exactly when black is no longer black and white no longer white. Our eye is easily fooled. Is the inner eye, that "sight" that looks inside to meditate, any more certain? Perhaps we can allow our perceptions of years to change. If so, views we've held for years can become transformed in a minute, and with them our world.

TUNISIAN LANDSCAPE, AUGUST MACKE

*Everything yields to success, even grammar.*
VICTOR HUGO

Meditation occurs when the reflective mind is at work in a highly focused, formal manner, which requires some degree of self-discipline. Paradoxically, in order to work reflectively, the mind must be in a restful state. Thus, meditation. In a meditative state we need not seek answers. We seek the freedom, the willingness if you will, to expand our awareness beyond our conscious thoughts and feelings. We open ourselves to new ideas, new possibilities, perhaps pieces of fantasies and dreams from unvisited, indeed unknown, as yet unexperienced times and places—the until-now-"unthought" thought, the "unknown" known—the other, endless paths to tranquility, creativity, spirituality, awareness, acceptance, and of course success. The word *success* has many meanings. In its original sense, success was defined as "that which ensues, outcome, consequence, issue." In other words it lacked a connotation of value and was simply the end product of an endeavor. Today we think of success as an accomplishment—attainment, prosperity, affluence, achievement, good fortune, fame, conquest, triumph, even victory. To find our own definition of success, we need to let our thoughts wander among the many images the word will summon when we allow the mind to traverse the boundaries between thought and feeling, reality and fantasy. Let us allow our thoughts the freedom to explore our inner unknown selves.

THE SLEEPING GYPSY, HENRI ROUSSEAU

*The excursion is the same when you go looking for your sorrow*
*as when you go looking for your joy.*

EUDORA WELTY

Once upon a time a little girl of three was given a beautiful Easter bunny by her grandmother. It was a big, soft, furry brown rabbit. The little girl loved her rabbit very much and even though the grandmother brought the child a different one every Easter as she grew older, she always loved the first rabbit best. The rabbit became her favorite toy in all the world, so naturally it went with her to the park. One sad day it disappeared. No one knows whether someone actually took it or if she and her mother forgot it, but when they returned to look for it just minutes later—and they did search high and low for many days after, asking everyone if it had been seen "accidentally" leaving with anyone else—it was most definitely gone. Every year the grandmother brought the girl another beautiful rabbit, but none ever became as important to her as the lost rabbit of her memory. And it was a *good* memory, even after it was gone, because the girl's mother had the wisdom to explain that whoever owned it now was possibly a child less fortunate than she, one who had never owned such a wonderful toy, maybe a little girl without a loving grandmother, to whom it must have brought great happiness. Perhaps we can all succeed in finding joy even as we experience sorrow by turning some of our bad memories into good ones. We can try to realize that "loss" doesn't only mean sorrow, that when we lose something we love, it can remain inside us as a good feeling, because while we still love it, we are at the same time sharing it if it has been found and loved by someone else.

MOTHER AND CHILD, MARY CASSATT

*It is not the answer that enlightens, but the question.*

EUGENE IONESCO

There seem to be a million ways in which we want to succeed as parents. One is to share our knowledge and experience of life and to answer our children's questions. Of course, we're not their only teachers, but our voices are surely the most influential. Do we unwittingly tend to tell them only what we want them to hear rather than what they want to know? The real questions that relate to what's actually happening in our children's lives tend to be complex, such as, "Mom, when the baby is born, will it be born in the egg or out of the egg?" and "How do you know that it will be born in nine months instead of nine weeks, like kittens, or two years, like elephants?" The basic "Where do babies come from?" can be difficult to explain, embarrassing maybe, but we manage. So far not too difficult for most of us. But what about later, when harder questions come up, questions about sex and gender, race and religion, persecution, politics, loss, death? Do we really listen to our children's concerns? Are we willing to answer these questions? Do we encourage their asking? Surely this is partly what it means to be a successful parent. Can we deal honestly, or at all, with any questions that challenge or put into doubt our own belief systems—about our political biases, our religious views, our moral and ethical standards? Let us take another look, and if not, perhaps ask ourselves why not?

CIRCULAR FORMS, SUN AND MOON, ROBERT DELAUNAY

*Dreams and visions are infused into men for their advantage and instruction.*

ARTEMIDORUS OF DALDIS

We hear a great deal about over-achieving and under-achieving, but little about what lies in the middle. Is that what we call mediocrity, or is being "average" of value? There is so much stress involved in what ought to be the simple business of growing up. Couldn't we make life less of a burden for ourselves as adults? We tend to view both the over- and under-achievers as emotionally or psychologically unhealthy, or out of balance. And certainly most children will go to any lengths to be the same as their peers, a child among children. So, why must we lose the dream as grown-ups to be "average," a worker among workers? As children, were we driven to excel at all costs? Can a woman be successful as a wife and mother, or must she have a high-powered career? Can she focus her energy on her home, children, and community and still view herself as successful? On the other hand, how many men are psychologically driven to exceed their father's career achievements for some obscure, yet real, emotional reason? And what about those men who are happiest staying home raising the children? Can they be viewed as successful? Will a "daddy track" ever become acceptable, a type of success even? We can allow ourselves the gift of freedom to develop and choose an average life, nurturing our dreams as they are, keeping the balance between work and home. Let us recognize that there is nothing mediocre in the happiness that comes as a result of a balanced life.

THE SEINE AT ASNIERES, PIERRE-AUGUSTE RENOIR

*Not in the clamor of the crowded street,*
*Not in the shouts and plaudits of the throng,*
*But in ourselves, are triumph and defeat.*

HENRY WADSWORTH LONGFELLOW

When our children bring home gold stars and "Excellent's" on their report cards, we of course applaud their success. But are we also instilling in them the idea that they must be perfect—the handsomest, the most popular, the most talented, among their peers? Are our messages full of the need for them to be the "greatest" or "highest"—the *est* words that can't come to pass without a lot of *shoulds* being instilled as well. Must they succeed at any cost?   And what is the effect on the less gifted or less accomplished sibling, the younger or older brother or sister who brings home only "Good's" or "Fair's" and silver stars, B's and C's instead of A's? Children develop in different ways, with various talents and capabilities, and at different speeds and times in their lives, some not coming into their own until they're beyond their school years. Are they not to be valued and loved also?   Do we love them above all, no matter what they do or don't accomplish? Can we permit, even encourage, them to *not* follow in our footsteps but rather to determine their own futures? Can we give them our unqualified emotional support whatever the outcome of their endeavors? Let us experience both their joys and their sorrows without judgment, criticism, or anger. Let us offer them the best of ourselves so that they may in turn experience the best of themselves.

YOUNG GIRLS AT PIANO, PIERRE-AUGUSTE RENOIR

*If one advances confidently in the direction of his dreams and endeavors to live the life which he has imagined, he will meet with a success unexpected in common hours.*
HENRY DAVID THOREAU

As children, we see only endless possibilities ahead of us. Time it seems, is eternal and no goal is unattainable. Suddenly twenty or thirty years have passed and none of what we were sure to have accomplished has been brought to fruition. We are coming to realize that what we wanted to do, wanted to be, are not necessarily what we *can* do or can be. Time is slipping away; we can't seem to catch up. Worse yet, we look around only to find that we seem to be the only ones not to have reached the place we were so sure to have reached by now. ■ It is easy for us to measure our own successes against those of our peers, but is it realistic, or even fair? How can I compare my progress to that of someone who hasn't experienced the events of my life? ■ Consider the addict who doesn't find her way into recovery until well into her thirties. Should she think herself a failure for not having a husband, two-and-a-half children, a home and two cars as her high school friends do . . . or at least a thriving career? Have they encountered the same obstacles, the same fortunes or misfortunes in their lives? ■ We understand that success is proportional to our life experience. And every success, be it earning a doctorate, winning the Nobel Prize, learning to drive a car or baking a pie, should be acknowledged. Perhaps waking up with a clear mind and conscience this morning deserves our gratitude today.

SUMMERTIME, JACKSON POLLOCK

*If a door slams shut, it means that God is pointing to an open door further on down.*
ANNA DELANEY PEALE

A man with a family to support may lose his job yet not have an inner sense of failure because he recognizes the success he achieved earlier in life. Perhaps he was validated for his efforts and accomplishments by his parents, friends, spouse or children. ▪ On the other hand, what if his spouse has not yet experienced her own unique value to those around her? Anticipating hardship in their future, she might view him as a failure indeed. Her fears may begin to chip away at his self-esteem. Perhaps he will begin to doubt his own worth, second-guess his strength and be lured into her fears of loss—of possessions and respect in the community. Perhaps together they will begin to doubt the validity of the marriage itself, losing their faith in the family unit as a stronghold against the vicissitudes of life. ▪ A happier possibility is that she, too, will have the strength and energy—born of her own self-esteem—to contribute "good" energy, if needed, to lift his flagging spirits to a place where motivation to go on will make a new beginning possible. ▪ Let us be prepared to let success in, to experience it in a way that can't be lost, to keep it stored for future use and be willing to reach down deep inside for the positive feelings needed to succeed in troubled times. Most important, let us be prepared to share our positive thoughts and feelings, our enthusiasm, when needed by those with whom we share our lives.

THE SOWER, VINCENT VAN GOGH

*To dry one's eyes and laugh at a fall*
*And baffled, get up and begin again.*
ROBERT BROWNING

Anyone seeking success on any level is at one time or another going to suffer a setback. Not only are falls inevitable, they are a necessary and vital part of our growth. In less severe cases, however, whether we choose to stay down wallowing in our pain or not is often up to us. ▪ What better expression of true resilience than that of a child at play? How many scraped knees have we breathlessly witnessed in the making as toddlers tripped over their feet on hard asphalt? And how many times are we amazed when, before we can even kiss away the hurt, their tears have dried and they're struggling to break free to get back to their friends? ▪ As we grow up, we find it increasingly difficult to spring back so readily. When we take a fall, our pain can't always be relieved by a mother's kiss and a smile. It seems that the more complex we become, the harder we fall and the deeper our pain. Is it possible that some of our smaller wounds appear bigger than they really are? Are we focusing too much time and energy on them when they really don't warrant such treatment? Can we realize that some things are handled better with less rather than more attention? ▪ Maybe as adults we can learn by watching children and try to recapture in ourselves some of the stamina and resilience that we see in them. We may find that by taking ourselves a little less seriously, we can lessen the effort of getting back up and back on our journey toward success.

THE OLIVE TREES, MAURICE DE VLAMINCK

*Blessed are they that mourn: for they shall be comforted.*

MATTHEW 5 : 4

To live successfully despite unhappiness seems paradoxical, since we equate "success" with positive emotions. However, it is just as important for our well-being to live through life's tragedies successfully as it is to achieve success in other arenas. We have all known families "surviving" the death of a loved one by stoically suppressing their deep feelings of sadness. They simply "keep a stiff upper lip" and go on. Depression and mourning are not part of their "sensible" way of life. Is it any wonder, then, that twenty years later they're still stuck in a swamp of despair, finding relief from their "unfelt" emotions in alcohol and drugs, mental illness, divorce, suicide? If parents don't allow themselves to experience their truly deep sadness, the children can't either, and must act out their emotions in self-destructive ways. They can't betray the big lie of "the happy family." What a pity, what a great waste, for all concerned. What happier lives they all might have lived. We must become willing to mourn, to let our sadness envelop us when it's there and real inside us, because it won't go away otherwise. Denial just begets more denial, whereas acceptance engenders truth. And acknowledging our own feelings, with all the guilt, frustration, powerlessness, and anger they may evoke, will lead us through our pain to the other side, perhaps to greater wisdom and strength. Happiness is not the only indicator of successful living. It is said that without pain there can be no growth, and surely growth is equated with success. Let us feel all of our feelings—and grow.

SUNRISE OFF THE MAINE COAST,
FREDERIC EDWIN CHURCH

*Socialists make the mistake of confusing individual worth with success.*
*They believe you cannot allow people to succeed in case those who fail feel worthless.*
KENNETH BAKER

Success! Such a troublesome concept. Do we have to become the most famous, the most accomplished, the wealthiest, in order to achieve it? Does the concert violinist have to be world-renowned? Does the actor have to become the top box-office star, the politician have to become president? Must every athlete break a record and win an Olympic gold medal, every lawyer become a Justice of the U.S. Supreme Court, every biologist discover the cure for the most devastating disease of her day? ■ Of course not! Every athletic record will eventually be broken. History alone tells us who the great politicians are. The lawyers who fight for the rights of the underdog are unlikely ever to attract enough attention to become judges on the highest court in the land. Do they experience themselves as failures because fame eludes them. Are working actors, who remain unknown but earn a good living, necessarily unfulfilled? Are "average" workers who, in fact, back up every Nobel Prize effort as part of a team, failures? Are the violinists who remain one of many in the orchestra not contributing to its success? ■ *Good! Better! Best!* All describe a degree of achievement, but determined by whom? Perhaps the "best" in success lies in the degree of effort and dedication we bring to our work. What is important is that we do our own best, and our sense of self-esteem and fulfillment tell us that we are doing just that. "Best," like success itself, lies in the eye of the beholder.

STILL LIFE WITH HEAD OF A RED BULL, PABLO PICASSO

*The common idea that success spoils people by making them vain, egotistic and self-complacent is erroneous; on the contrary, it makes them, for the most part, humble, tolerant, and kind. Failure makes people cruel and bitter.*

W. SOMERSET MAUGHAM

Human behavior has been charted and documented by numerous highly respected studies, but in the past, researchers have focused primarily on men. Only now have men *and* women, boys *and* girls been studied comparatively—to reveal that we differ socially in a number of important ways that contribute greatly to defining our behaviors through life. It seems clear in the area of human relations, boys are programmed to solve problems by winning, whereas girls are equally socialized to solve problems with the desired outcome of harmony and friendship, even among competitors. Whatever the reasons for this difference in our natures, it does exist. Yet women tend to want and expect men to be like them in such areas as the experience of empathy, parenting styles and so on. Indeed many men do meet these expectations, but there are also men who retain traditional views equating success primarily with earning power, which many of us seem to frown upon today. Who is to say that money, prestige, and power should not be important to a man—or a woman, for that matter—that he (or she) should not strive to be the best that he can be on *whatever* path his talents and interests take him, that he should not take pride in supporting his family well, focusing on achievement and recognition? Let us view men—lovers, husbands, sons, and fathers—as motivated not by the meanness of ambition, but by the joy of achieving self-expression and self-worth.

RED MAY, SANDOR BORTNYK

*In order that people may be happy in their work, these three things are needed:*
*They must be fit for it. They must not do too much of it.*
*And they must have a sense of success in it.*

JOHN RUSKIN

Not achieving one's goal need not necessarily translate into failure. Is the actor responsible for how critics of differing opinions view his performance? Is the entrepreneur who has invested all his time, money, and energy in a business responsible for an unexpected recession that may undermine his efforts before he even starts . . . or are the newlyweds who have so carefully chosen a safe building site responsible when they lose their home to a flood or hurricane? ▪ Having our plans or dreams come to an abrupt halt is upsetting and disappointing, but when we internalize as our own personal failure a situation that has gone awry due to external forces, we can find ourselves trapped within the confines of hopelessness and discouragement, weakened and without motivation to move on. ▪ Taking responsibility for the choices we make, knowing we've done everything we can to the very best of our ability may help us get past self-blame, anger, and depression. Then we may be more inclined to perceive these experiences not as failures but as unavoidable losses. Farther on down the road, we may even come to see that there was much to be learned from such painful lessons. ▪ Let us, then, understand that true success lies in our ability to accept, overcome, learn, and grow from the hardships we endure throughout our lifetimes, and let us value our honest efforts, whatever the results.

RESTAURANT DE LA MACHINE A BOUGIVAL,
MAURICE DE VLAMINCK

*There is nothing more difficult to take in hand, more perilous to conduct, or more uncertain in its success, than to take the lead in the introduction of a new order of things.*

NICCOLO MACHIAVELLI

The women's movement, which addresses itself to equality, especially in the workplace, is a powerful example of "the introduction of a new order of things," and women, just like men, wish their changing goals and aspirations to be viewed with respect, compassion, and understanding. ■ Hardly a week goes by without a new book being published emphasizing our differences in all areas from communication styles to life goals. Still, we all rightfully acknowledge that justice includes equality between the sexes. So, how do we resolve the paradox of different yet the same, different yet equally valuable, different yet fairly judged? ■ We already know that men can perform domestic and parenting duties as well as women, and that women can perform roles in industry at all levels, be it in a scientist's laboratory, at an investment banking firm, or on an automotive assembly line. Yet, many people—even women—cling to the old vision of women as inappropriate or less able in many work areas. ■ Yes, change is always difficult, but let us also recall the words of Marcus Aurelius—"The universe is change, life is understanding"—and examine our biases in these matters. Are we striving to dissolve these discriminatory feelings that have been so deeply a part of our culture? Can we permit true regard and respect for women and their chosen goals to enter our minds and our relationships?

ODALISQUE A LA CULOTTE ROUGE, HENRI MATISSE

*A musician must make music, an artist must paint, a poet must write,*
*if he is to be ultimately at peace with himself. What a man can be, he must be.*
ABRAHAM MASLOW

Remember the rhyme we recited as children, "Rich man, poor man, beggar man, thief; Doctor, lawyer, Indian chief," bouncing a ball or jumping rope until we "missed" in order to determine our future? As adults, do we still believe that luck holds the answer—or is there a more successful way of choosing our field of endeavor, of experiencing our calling? ■ Do we believe in a hierarchy among professions, a better/best equation? Is the farmer better than the doctor, the teacher, or the man of God who chooses poverty as his way of life? If there is a contest, who wins, and who decides who wins? Is the leader better than the follower, the teacher better than the student? We must do what we can do, and what we can do is determined by the intelligence, temperament, and talents with which we were born, and by the environment in which we were raised—the family myths, the times in which we live. We begin with those basics, and how we use them depends on our own motivation and ambition. ■ For some of us the goals are clear. For others there will be many excursions into different fields before finding the one that is satisfying. For still others the whole of life is a search for the right path. Perhaps the only answers lie within the spiritual part of ourselves, where we attempt to suspend judgement. Let us try to find the generosity of spirit to accept *all* the paths as potential paths to success.

MONET IN HIS STUDIO BOAT, EDOUARD MANET

*The man of virtue makes the difficulty to be overcome his first business,*
*and success only a subsequent consideration.*

CONFUCIUS

For some of us success and fulfillment mean achieving a quiet, consistent, dependable lifestyle. Others seek a more daring lifestyle, and thrive on the thrill of exploring the unknown, taking risks, and seek success in every challenge to be met and obstacle to be overcome. Take for example, the life of the entrepreneur. Such people must be willing not only to take risks, but often to invest everything they have in risky ventures. Or consider the precarious path of the writer or actor. As artists they leave themselves open to an endless amount of rejection before having a publisher or producer or the general public accept their work. Believing in ourselves requires deep faith at times. Can we stay committed to our goals without losing that faith and confidence in ourselves and our abilities? Any decision to challenge the odds, even at the risk of self-sacrifice, requires courage. The ability to keep going in the face of adversity requires conviction. Regardless of the outcome, do we recognize our sense of courage and conviction as success in and of itself? Let us stay true to our own selves, and rely on our strength of heart and inner resolve in our pursuit of whatever form of success it is we seek in life.

WATERCOLOUR COMPOSITION, OTTO FREUNDLICH

*There is more to life than increasing its speed.*
MAHATMA GANDHI

We often use the word burnout in reference to our jobs. The dictionary defines it as (a) "The breakdown of an electrical device due to excessive heat created by the current flowing through it"; and (b) "exhaustion." It is a concept that can apply to every area of our lives and, when not held in check, can not only impede progress but can bring it to a screeching halt entirely, thereby blocking any degree of success. ▪ Consider the long-distance runner. When running a marathon does he reach the finish line in his best time by sprinting the first five miles? Hardly. To do so would result in oxygen deprivation, forcing him to slow down while trying to gain it back, and would ultimately increase rather than decrease his overall running time. Or look at the person who, carrying a full-time job and raising a family, decides to return to school and enrolls in a full-time study program. While the objective is admirable—to embark on a more profitable, fulfilling profession—it is possible that overload and eventually burnout will lead to "dropout" and defeat. ▪ There are some who can burn the candle successfully at both ends, but most of us need to set a more moderate pace. When we spread ourselves too thin, we defeat our own purpose. No task gets our full attention, and the results are likely to be just okay rather than the best we can do. After all, success isn't found in the quantity of our endeavors, but in the quality of all we achieve in our lifetime.

LA SIESTE, VINCENT VAN GOGH

*In each of us there is another whom we do not know.*
*He speaks to us in dreams and tells us how*
*differently he sees us from the way we see ourselves.*

CARL GUSTAV JUNG

What is the appeal of a good mystery or thriller? Most would agree that the allure of such stories lies in the suspense, the unexpected twists, and surprise endings. Viewing ourselves as authors of our own "life script," are we willing to entertain fresh ideas, to stray from the beaten path of the expected and to venture forth into unknown territories, welcoming adventure and newness into our lives? Is it possible that each story may have more than one ending? Or are we stuck in the quagmire of repetition and predictability? While it may be true that we are creatures of habit, it is also true that as thinking, feeling human beings we possess within us the power to break or change those habits. If we chose to do so, we might create for ourselves a life filled with enough freshness to keep us looking forward to turning the page. In our search, then, for the experience of success, when we find ourselves feeling bound and tethered by the usual and the expected, let's break the chains of familiarity and predictable outcomes and instead seek the excitement, vitality, and infinite possibilities that a little daring and openness can lend to life. In so doing, perhaps we shall find ourselves authors of increasingly exciting and surprising chapters of our own life stories.

OLD HOUSES IN LINDAU, RUDOLF WACKER

*We have a problem. Congratulations.*

*But it's a tough problem. Then double congratulations.*

W .   C L E M E N T   S T O N E

Recently a friend accepted a job, one of those jobs that keeps the wolf from the door, pays the rent, and buys the food. Granted, it had little to do with his true career goals. What it did have to do with was survival in the "cold, cruel world" while he became a successful writer and waited for the great novel (or play—whatever) to appear at the end of his pen. At the last minute the job fell through. It simply wasn't there, at least not for my friend. ■ Fair? Hardly! But then, I'm not sure what fair is. Is there any "fair" in life? They say, and I'm not sure who "they" are, that God only gives you what you can handle. When stuck somewhere between anger, depression, and self-pity, it is easy to perceive the seemingly "unfair" minor setbacks in life as tragic events. But how does anyone dealing with *real* tragedy feel about "fair"? How do the hungry and the homeless, the sick and the dying, feel about "fair"? That makes self-pity seem inappropriate. ■ There will be another job, there always is. In getting through small difficulties we realize that we all have the gifts of acceptance, perseverance, faith, and trust somewhere inside us, attitudes that, if we choose to rely on them, perhaps will get us through this day. Let us have gratitude for the gift of life and the motivation to live it, to go on no matter what.

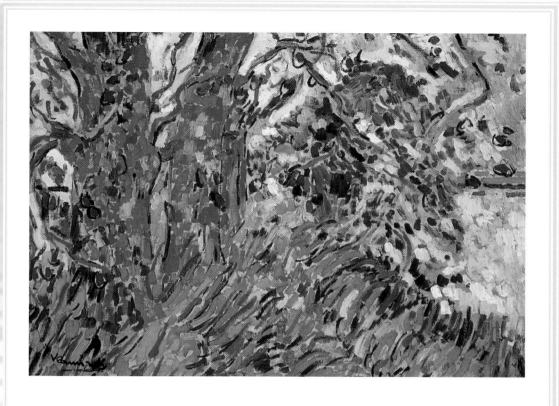

BANK OF THE SEINE AT CHÂTOUX,
MAURICE DE VLAMINCK

*Where there is patience and humility, there is neither anger nor vexation.*

SAINT FRANCIS OF ASSISI

I f we think of success in terms of reaching our desired destination, think of all the time wasted on just being lost when we could have stopped and asked directions along the way. Perhaps pride and vanity were the controlling factors, when humility and modesty would have served us better.     Whatever the reasons—a need to be in control, a lack of faith in the competence of others, a need to prove something to the world with an "I can do it myself" attitude, or not wanting to appear to be weak—many of us have difficulty seeking help or guidance along the way. When we look at what lies beneath our Herculean tendencies, don't we find that feelings of grandiosity and our own self-will are really the governing forces and self-defeating ones at that?     Finding humility within ourselves doesn't come easily for everyone. But undeniably, without some degree of it we are bound to find ourselves moving farther away rather than closer to our desired destinations.     So the next time we find ourselves lost, be it physically, mentally, or spiritually, we might try pulling over and asking for directions. Then and only then shall we realize that seeking guidance can not only expedite our getting to where we wish to be, but can help us experience a deeper understanding of humility and the power it offers in ensuring a safe and successful journey through life.

LANDSCAPE AT CHÂTOUX, MAURICE DE VLAMINCK

*You gain strength, courage and confidence by every experience*
*in which you really stop to look fear in the face.*
*You are able to say to yourself, "I lived through this horror.*
*I can take the next thing that comes along . . ."*

ELEANOR ROOSEVELT

When caught in the suffocating grip of fear, we feel our chances of succeeding at even the smallest task slipping farther from our grasp. Like a deer frozen in headlights, we find ourselves virtually immobilized, so overwhelmed are we by fear's powerful effect on us. Blocking out the light of reason, it leaves us floundering in the darkness, robbing us of hope and faith, and filling us with despair. ▦ For many of us it is the smaller everyday problems that, when ignored long enough, snowball into feelings of panic, even desperation. Feeding our denial by stuffing unpaid bills in the drawer or cutting class when we're not prepared for an exam only fuels our fears. When these minor problems then reach the realm of the impossible, we wonder why we are unable to cope. ▦ Our impulse to resist our feelings of fear is as natural a part of the human condition as fear itself. Yet how do we face that which we are unwilling to see? Admitting we're afraid and knowing it's okay to be afraid is half the battle. Just letting these feelings in defuses them. ▦ Let us find our success in the knowledge that there is courage, strength, and hope even in darkness. For, in the words of Charles Beard, "When it is dark enough, you can see the stars."

COMPOSITION, OTTO FREUNDLICH

*To go against one's conscience is neither safe nor right.*

*Here I stand. I cannot do otherwise.*

MARTIN LUTHER

Having the courage of our convictions in the face of overwhelming odds is perhaps the most difficult form of success to achieve, but possibly the most gratifying. History is full of martyrs who died for their beliefs. Few of us have had to make such weighty decisions, but we do sometimes have to stand and fight for our beliefs. George Bernard Shaw said, "This is the true joy in life, the being used for a purpose recognized by yourself as a mighty one. . . ." What do we ordinary mortals view as mighty purposes and just causes, and what are the risks we take in defending them? Our battles, for example, might be fought in the arena of equal rights and respect, or some change that seems essential to our own or our children's well-being. There are endless possibilities. Along the way we might lose friends who disagree with us, and pride as we are sometimes proved wrong, but those risks are acceptable if we're to stand up to our beliefs. Let us all try to have the courage of our convictions when it's important and to be willing to bend when it's not—and to find our strength in re-membering those who've gone that step farther—Martin Luther King, John and Robert Kennedy, Mahatma Gandhi, to name but a few—who gave their lives for what they believed to be in the interest of all. Let us remember also that success lies not nec-essarily in winning but in making our most honest, unstinting effort.

HOUSES ON A HILL, PABLO PICASSO

*The bird is in the sky, the stone rests on the land.*
*In water lives the fish, my spirit in God's hand.*
ANGELUS SILESIUS

When it comes to the spiritual side of life, we have been given a range of choices. Those of us who are fiercely independent, with a strong belief in free will tend to minimize the importance of spirituality. However, we may feel less alone if we allow ourselves to believe in a Higher Power who guides and protects us. Belief in the Higher Power requires faith, and that *is* belief. It's a simple paradox requiring no proof or understanding, just the taking of that leap. ■ Belief in God can give us respite from the constant struggle to have to understand. The atheist is burdened with that need, seeking alternative explanations to creation, life, the universe—in short, everything—because there is no God. For the agnostic the burden is a bit lighter, for he or she contends that the essential nature of things is both unknown and unknowable. ■ But for most of us it is more meaningful to accept a path of belief that brings comfort, hope, perhaps some help in defining life's rules, one that offers a value system by which to live without our having to figure everything out—one that brings us back to faith. ■ If the successful path is one that does not presuppose total free will and absolute independence, and instead embraces faith (perhaps the softer way) then that path lies in spirituality. The choice is ours.

LOOKING OUT AT SACRE-COEUR,
PIERRE-AUGUSTE RENOIR

*Man is a complex being. He makes deserts bloom—and lakes die.*

GIL STERN

Beyond the tangible, more immediate, personal successes we think about, strive toward, and experience in our daily lives, there is another, more far-reaching goal we all share. That goal is to ensure the survival of *our* home for *our* children—*our* planet. While great strides have been made in raising public awareness on environmental issues, there unfortunately remains a vast percentage of us who can't or won't see beyond our own lifetime, our own needs and comforts, dreams and aspirations. Can we allow our shortsightedness to hinder the potential for a thriving, flourishing tomorrow? As the highest order of species (at least to date) in the process of evolution, don't we bear a responsibility to nurture and maintain the life-giving forces that nature offers us? Can we deny that there is success to be found in keeping the ecological balance and living in harmony with our natural surroundings? If we can turn our focus from the "here and now" to the "here and future," and expand our sense of place in the world, perhaps then we can pass on to our children the legacy left to us by our ancestors, the gift of life itself. Let us share a vision of the future and become willing to put forth the extra effort today, so that our children may see and enjoy the fruits of our labor tomorrow.

VILLAGE 1906, MAURICE DE VLAMINCK

*In our springtime everyday has its hidden growth in the mind,*
*as it has in the earth when the little folded blades*
*are getting ready to pierce the ground.*

GEORGE ELIOT

During the course of our lives we can encounter innumerable successes, some big, some small, some external, some internal. Those that come to us internally—new self-awareness, self-discovery—are those that are apt to slip by more easily, unnoticed and unacknowledged for the true significance and value they hold in our lives. For a stargazer, enlightenment is seeing the heavens through a telescope for the first time. As the moon's surface suddenly fills the field of vision, what had previously been just a beautiful object in the sky to sleep and dream under suddenly becomes connected to one's own personal "universe" here on Earth. It gives a profound gift—a new sense of self and a heightened awareness of one's own place in the cosmos. Enlightenment is an internal experience. It happens as we gain knowledge of ourselves and the world around us, giving rise to a higher consciousness and deeper level of understanding. Then when we walk under a clear nighttime sky, we can relive that stargazer's moment. As we encounter moments of self-awareness, do we stop to appreciate them? Are we able to acknowledge the true value of the gift of clarity of vision, of revelation? If not, perhaps we should, for it is in the light of newfound awareness that we can truly see and experience the success of the moment and our growing sense of self.

LES NYMPHEAS, CLAUDE MONET

*Crossing a bare common, in snow puddles, at twilight under a clouded sky,*
*without having in my thoughts any occurrence of special good fortune,*
*I have enjoyed a perfect exhilaration. I am glad to the brink of fear.*

RALPH WALDO EMERSON

Finding the experience of success through meditation when we're in the unlikely realm of defeat, failure, fear, or sorrow is a valuable achievement. Of course we're prepared to experience successful feelings when fame, fortune, love, and happiness come our way, for that's just where we expect these feelings to be. ▦ Surprisingly, "everyday" success can be found, too, in every little pocket, every nook and cranny, of life—tiny lights waiting to be turned into bright flames when time stops for us and we are still enough to be touched by them. Success is when . . . our cat comes when we whistle, we clean the closets, we recognize the composer of a classical piece of music on the radio, we hold a baby, we finish what we start (sometimes success is just getting started), we get out to vote even in a blizzard, we manage to enjoy a rock n' roll concert with a teenager, we complete our marathon run even though it's not a "personal best," we love the ones we love when it's really hard, and we let them love us in their own way. ▦ Success is . . . improbable, endless subjects for our meditations. These understandings remain inside us, ready to be revealed whenever we are ready to open our minds and hearts to them. We may even stumble across them in our dreams. Let us open to them, and experience them in all the times, all of the days and nights, of our lives.

TWILIGHT ON THE SHAWANGUNK,
WHITTREDGE WORTHINGTON

*Zen does not confuse spirituality with thinking about God while one is peeling potatoes. Zen spirituality is just to peel the potatoes.*

ALAN WATTS

Many of us are confused about spirituality and how to let it enter into our lives and become something more than just words to us. One way is to start each day trusting in the promise it may hold. Do any of us really have to get up on the wrong side of bed and go through the day making ourselves and others miserable? Realistic anxiety may fuel a bad mood, but need we hang on to it? Can balance and serenity be restored? Yes, we can successfully retrieve the good side of ourselves by loving and being supportive of our loved ones. We can take the time for prayer and meditation daily, which will ward off most of our fears, and find a few minutes to do so again should we feel overwhelmed during the day. We might establish the habit of seeking sanctuary in a quiet, cloistered space without a particular need to find help or solve a problem, only the desire to experience quiet inside and out. We might try to help another person in distress, taking the focus off ourselves and our problems. Most important, let's take responsibility for the conduct of our own lives, make every sensible effort to solve our problems, and then have the sense to let go, suspend judgment of ourselves and let our spirituality truly take over. Perhaps then we can, at the end of the day, sleep peacefully knowing that we've done our best, knowing that the rest is up to God.

L'ESTAQUE ON THE GULF OF MARSEILLE, FRANCE,
PAUL CEZANNE

## PERMISSIONS AND ACKNOWLEDGEMENTS

Grateful acknowledgement is made to Art Resource and Erich Lessing/Art Resource, Giraudon/Art Resource, Tate Gallery, Superstock, and The Granger Collection, for permission to use the works of art printed herein.

Grateful acknowledgement is made to Artists' Rights Society for permission to use the works of art herein.

Grateful acknowledgement is made to W. Clement Stone Enterprises, Lake Forest, Illinois 60045, for permission to reprint words by Mr. W. Clement Stone. All rights for the World administered by W. Clement Stone Enterprises.